anxiety
is my
sidekick

anxiety is my sidekick

A JOURNAL FOR FEELING ALL THE FEELINGS

CHRONICLE BOOKS
San Francisco

ISBN 978-1-7972-1021-6

Manufactured in China.

MIX
Paper from
responsible sources
FSC™ C104723

Design by **Vanessa Dina**.

This journal is in no way intended as a substitute for the medical
advice of physicians or therapists. If you seek to treat a mental and/
or physical condition using journaling, please consult with your
physician or a licensed healthcare provider first.

10 9 8 7 6 5 4 3 2 1

Chronicle Books LLC
680 Second Street
San Francisco, California 94107
www.chroniclebooks.com

Welcome to **Anxiety Is My Sidekick**, a calming companion for difficult moments and a safe space to share your thoughts.

Journaling is an act of self-care; research shows that a regular journaling practice can reduce stress and promote well-being. This journal is designed to help you manage stress, worry, and anxiety by giving you space to organize and process your feelings on a daily basis. Putting your feelings on paper will allow you to see things more clearly, understand what triggers difficult emotions, and help you set positive intentions so that you're better able to manage stress the next time it comes up.

In the following pages, you'll find blank space to vent, make lists, record calming experiences, set joyful goals, and write about whatever else you need to process. You'll also find soothing mantras and calming phrases offering inspiration and support so that you can welcome each day with hope, courage, and peace.

This is your space. Feel your feelings. Take care of yourself.

Release what you cannot control.

Close your eyes. Take a deep breath. Hold for three seconds. Then let it all go.

What does the best version of tomorrow look like?

Be gentle with yourself. You're doing the best you can.

Say "no" to something that's making you feel overwhelmed.

When fear or anxiety bubbles up, notice those feelings without judgment. Imagine they are clouds passing in the sky.

Your worries, stresses, and anxieties do not define you.

How can you be kinder to yourself?

Write yourself a love letter.

Think of five things that make you smile.

Focus on what's going right.

Think of a challenge you've faced. How did you use your strength to overcome that experience?

Think of a memory that makes you smile. Next time you feel overwhelmed,

close your eyes and tune in to that moment, recalling it in as much detail as possible.

Inhale calm, exhale worry.

This too shall pass.

What does stress feel like in your body? Next time stressful feelings arise,

breathe deeply and send your breath to those areas with love and kindness.

What's one thing you can do today to make yourself feel good? Do it.

Celebrate today's small victories.

Visualize a place that brings you peace in as much detail as possible. Call on that image when you feel anxious.

When you feel yourself getting anxious about the future, take a deep breath and tune in to the present moment.

Feel the ground beneath your feet, listen to the sounds around you. Be here now.

What can you let go of today?

Think of someone who makes you feel calm. When anxious thoughts arise, imagine they are holding your hand.